Little People, BIG DREAMS®
CRISTIANO RONALDO

Written by
Maria Isabel Sánchez Vegara

Illustrated by
João Fazenda

Frances Lincoln
Children's Books

On the Portuguese island of Madeira lived a boy called Cristiano who spent his days kicking around an old ball. His family didn't have much, but football gave him hope. He dreamt of playing at the club where his dad worked.

Before long, Cristiano earned a spot on the club's junior team. He hated losing so much that he cried every time it happened. Some kids laughed at him, but he knew it was okay to have big feelings. It showed how much he cared.

At ten, Cristiano joined Nacional, the number-one team on the island. He trained with quiet determination and soon became the team's captain. Sometimes he was asked to play with boys much older, and even then he stood out.

Two years later, news of Cristiano's talent crossed the sea and reached Lisbon, the capital of Portugal. He was excited to sign for one of the country's biggest clubs — but leaving his family behind was so hard that he almost gave up.

Luckily, Cristiano chose to stay at Sporting. He trained and played with such drive that, at just sixteen, he became one of the youngest to join the first team. But he wouldn't stay there for long . . .

To celebrate the opening of their brand-new stadium, Sporting hosted a friendly match against Manchester United. Cristiano played so well that on their flight home, the Manchester United players begged their coach to sign him.

Cristiano arrived in Manchester with flashy boots and fancy footwork. Some teammates weren't sure what to make of him. But in no time, he was scoring goals and winning titles – and at twenty-three, he was named the best player in the world.

When Real Madrid signed Cristiano, eighty-thousand fans filled the stadium just to see him wearing their jersey. CR7, as everyone would call him, was ready to shine at one of the most legendary teams in the world.

For almost ten years, he scored more goals than anyone in Real Madrid's history. He also led the team to over fifteen major titles – including four Champions League trophies in just five seasons, something no club had ever done before.

Yet Cristiano hoped to take his country just as far. He helped Portugal win the European Championship – their first major trophy. But the chance to lift the World Cup slipped away, over and over again.

After years in Spain, Cristiano moved to Italy to play for Juventus, then made a hero's return to Manchester United, before heading to Saudi Arabia. Yet it was at home, playing for Portugal, that he scored his 900th goal – a world record!

But beyond the fame, the luxury and the glamour that surrounded his life and family, Cristiano quietly cared for others.

He donated to hospitals, supported children's charities and never forgot what it felt like to grow up with very little.

And with every goal he scored, little Cristiano – the boy with an old ball and a giant dream – showed that the biggest journeys can begin in the smallest places.

CRISTIANO RONALDO

(Born 1985)

2003

2009

Born in Funchal, Portugal, Cristiano Ronaldo is one of the greatest athletes in football history. His father worked for Andorinha football club and introduced Cristiano to the sport early on. When Cristiano started playing professionally he soon joined Sporting Clube de Portugal – one of Portugal's best clubs. His talent was spotted by major European teams, and in 2003, Cristiano signed with Manchester United in a record deal for a player his age. Fans weren't sure about this new player with 'fancy footwork'. But his talent shone, and he helped Manchester United win three Premier League titles. In 2009, Cristiano moved to Real Madrid where he continued to delight fans with his skill and commitment. He became Real Madrid's all-time top scorer. Looking for a new challenge, he moved to

2019   2025

the Italian club, Juventus, in 2018. He ended his time with them by winning the Capocannoniere award – making him the first player to be top scorer in the English, Spanish and Italian leagues. After a brief return to Manchester United in 2021, Cristiano moved to the Saudi Arabian club, Al-Nassr. Cristiano's career is filled with incredible record-breaking achievements, including playing in 197 UEFA Champions League matches. One of his happiest moments was becoming Portugal's captain and helping the team win the European Championship. Off the pitch, he was named the world's most charitable sportsperson in 2015. From humble beginnings to becoming a world-famous football legend, Cristiano shows us that through hard work, dedication and heart, anything is possible.

Want to find out more about **Cristiano Ronaldo?**

Have a read of this great book:

Ronaldo Rules (Football Superstars) by Simon Mugford

Text © 2026 Maria Isabel Sánchez Vegara. Illustrations © 2026 João Fazenda
Original idea of the series by Maria Isabel Sánchez Vegara, published by Alba Editorial, S.L.U
"Little People, BIG DREAMS" and "Pequeña & Grande" are trademarks of
Alba Editorial S.L.U. and/or Beautifool Couple S.L.
First Published in the UK in 2026 by Frances Lincoln Children's Books, an imprint of The Quarto Group.
1 Triptych Place, London, SE1 9SH, United Kingdom. T 020 7700 6700 www.Quarto.com
EEA Representation, WTS Tax d.o.o., Žanova ulica 3, 4000 Kranj, Slovenia. www.wts-tax.si
All rights reserved.
No part of this publication may be reproduced, stored in a retrieval system, or transmitted, in any form,
or by any means, electrical, mechanical, photocopying, recording or otherwise without the prior written
permission of the publisher or a licence permitting restricted copying.

This book is not authorised, licensed or approved by Cristiano Ronaldo.
Any faults are the publisher's who will be happy to rectify for future printings.
A catalogue record for this book is available from the British Library.
ISBN 978-1-80570-170-5
Set in Futura BT.

Published by Juliet Matthews · Designed by Sasha Moxon, Izzy Bowman and Karissa Santos
Edited by Lucy Menzies and Claire Grace · Editorial management by Izzie Hewitt
Production by Robin Boothroyd
Manufactured in Shanghai, China CC122025
1 3 5 7 9 8 6 4 2

Photographic acknowledgements (pages 28-29, from left to right): 1. Cristiano Ronaldo of Manchester United runs with the ball during the FA Barclaycard Premiership match between Newcastle United and Manchester United, held on 23rd August, 2003, at St James' Park, in Newcastle, England. (Photo by Stu Forster/Getty Images.) 2. New Real Madrid player Cristiano Ronaldo is presented at the Santiago Bernabéu stadium on 6th July, in Madrid, Spain. (Photo by Denis Doyle/Getty Images.) 3. Cristiano Ronaldo of Portugal during the UEFA Euro 2020 Qualifier between Luxembourg and Portugal on 17th November, 2019, in Luxembourg, Luxembourg. (Photo by TF-Images/Getty Images.) 4. Captain Cristiano Ronaldo gets ready to lift the trophy, as Portugal celebrate winning the tournament for a second time after the UEFA Nations League Final 2025 between Portugal and Spain at Munich Football Arena on 8th June, 2025, in Munich, Germany. (Photo by Alexandra Fechete/MB Media/Getty Images.)